Greek
and
Roman
Pottery
Lamps

Donald M. Bailey

Greek and Roman Pottery Lamps

PUBLISHED BY

The Trustees of the British Museum

1972

Reprinted in Great Britain
at the University Press, Oxford
by Vivian Ridler
Printer to the University

Contents

Introduction

*This booklet illustrates various types of pottery lamps made
mainly in the Mediterranean world from the Minoan period until
early Christian times.*

*Such lamps can be very attractive small objects and well repay
attention. They are of interest to the social and art historian
because of the representations of daily life, religion and mythology,
and of lost masterpieces of sculpture appearing on some Roman
lamps. Lamps are useful, too, to the archaeologist in that they are
ephemeral and are easily recognisable: even small fragments can
be placed within their types. These types can, on the whole, be
dated comparatively closely, and so, in lamps, the excavator has a
valuable dating tool. The distribution of lamps foreign to the area
in which they are found is some indication of the pattern of trade
in the ancient world, while the various uses to which lamps were
put illustrate aspects of social and religious life.*

*Owing to space limitations, only a few of the thousands of lamps
in the Museum's collections can be described or illustrated here,
and only a limited number are displayed in the public galleries for
the same reason. Most of the Antiquities Departments possess
pottery lamps, and these can normally be made available to
interested members of the public if notice is given.*

*I would like to thank Mr D. E. L. Haynes and Mr R. A. Higgins
for reading the text and making many useful observations; also
Mr Lukas A. Benachi, Professor P. E. Corbett, Miss Judith
Perlzweig, and Mr A. F. Shore, who, over many years, have
furnished me with much invaluable information, and Miss Kathleen
Kenyon for details of Palestinian lamps. Special thanks are due
to Dr D. E. Strong, who read the text and proofs, and whose
advice and encouragement I have sought on many matters,
always with helpful results.*

The physical requirements of pottery lamps are simple: a container for the fuel, the fuel itself, a wick to enable the fuel to burn and to feed the fuel to the flame, and a continuous air supply. These are basic; all other aspects of lamps are refinements and improvements.

A wick floating in a bowl of oil will burn where it surfaces, but the flame cannot be controlled, and will produce smoke as well as light. A minor improvement is to channel the wick by pinching-in the rim of the bowl, as in the 'cocked-hat' lamps (pls. 1, c, d), but this still leaves a considerable length of the wick clear of the oil. The introduction of the bridged nozzle was a definite advance, as only the end of the wick appears at the wick-hole, and the flame produced can be tamped down until it is virtually smoke-less. The nozzle on early lamps was, generally speaking, very short, barely projecting from the wide, open bowl. As lamps developed, and the oil container became more enclosed and deeper, aesthetically a longer nozzle would fit more happily on the lamp.

Moulded lamps, when introduced, followed closely the shape and nozzle length of the contemporary wheel-made lamps, but during Roman times the nozzle shortened once more until in the 3rd and later centuries A.D. the wick-hole in some lamps was in effect pierced through the shoulder, the nozzle almost merging with the body. A long nozzle would not appear to be a great utilitarian improvement; variations are, in the main, due to a local fashion and taste: at all periods, where one area preferred a long nozzle, a short nozzle was favoured elsewhere.

The gradual closing-in of the body or oil container was, on the other hand, very practical. The fuel was less likely to spill or dry up, it hindered rats and mice drinking the oil, and insects, attracted by the light, would not so easily fall in and drown. Inserting and adjusting the wick was rather less easy, however, but the slight extra trouble in this respect was obviously out-weighed by the many advantages.

Handles, although not a necessary feature, appear on Minoan lamps, and on the earliest Athenian lamps of the 7th century B.C. Their use is largely a matter of local or temporal taste, some areas and periods favouring them more than others.

Bases merely allowed the lamp to stand steadily: turned bases are not usually found on the wide 'cocked-hat' lamps, nor upon some of the shallow open Greek examples, but most wheel-made lamps have a well-defined base. Moulded lamps, also, are nor-mally provided with an adequate base or base ring.

Pottery lamps are a cheap and practical means of illumination, easy to produce, handle and use, but are rather messy in operation. Oil oozes from the wick-hole in greater quantities than the flame

can burn, and runs down the outside of the lamp. This oozing probably explains the number of lamp-holders found in Britain: as oil had to be imported, wastage was to be avoided. Oil collected in the holders after some hours of burning could be poured back into the lamp. A lamp produces a fairly reasonable light – about the same as that from a candle (but requires less attention: the wick does not have to be snuffed, but very gradually burns away, needing to be pulled forward occasionally with a needle or tweezers). When tamped down, the flame produces little or no smoke, but a larger and brighter flame can be obtained by pulling out the wick slightly, although an oily black smoke results.

Brighter smokeless lights were made possible only by an increase in the number of lamps used together or by increasing the number of nozzles on a lamp. Two-wick lamps are very common, and many lamps with up to a dozen nozzles have been found. Exceptional lamps, often found in sanctuaries, can have several hundred wicks. Two wicks will, of course, burn twice as much oil as a single-nozzled lamp, and giant lamps with several nozzles (pl. 5a) have a large container to ensure that replenishing with oil was not required too often. The length of time a lamp will burn also depends on the size of the wick. An experiment showed that one fluid ounce of olive oil burned for over three hours, using a linen wick of small calibre, while a fatter wick burned for half that time; there was not much difference in the size of the flame in these two cases, but a really substantial wick, such as would be required by the lamp shown on pl. 8a would produce a large but perhaps smoky flame.

Wicks and Fuel

Wicks were made from any available fibrous material which would, by capillary action, suck the fuel from the container and deliver it to the wick-hole. Substances used for wicks in Roman lamps included linen, papyrus, mullein, oakum, fibres of the castor plant, and perhaps asbestos.

The fuel used in ancient lamps, like the material of the wicks, depended largely on availability – olive oil was probably the principal fuel employed in most Mediterranean countries, and was exported to areas where the olive did not grow. Britain, for instance, would have to obtain all olive oil used from abroad. Other oils which were probably used in lamps include sesame oil (mainly in the East), nut oil, fish oil, castor oil and other plant oils. Crude, surface-occurring mineral oil was perhaps used, when obtainable, in Mesopotamia. Except for the latter, it must be remembered that when burning oil in lamps one is actually

burning food, so only societies producing a food surplus could afford to use lamps extensively, and areas which had to import edible oils would be inclined to use them for cooking rather than fuel. This probably accounts for the comparatively few lamps found in Britain.

Uses of Lamps

Although we can be sure that daylight governed life to a far greater extent than at the present time, in antiquity lamps were used by every stratum of society, the poorer people using the common wheel-made and mould-made lamps, and the richer their elaborate metal examples. Houses were lit poorly or brightly according to the owner's circumstances. The many mining enterprises necessary for supplying the basic material requirements of the ancient world needed illumination, and lamp niches are a common feature in shafts and galleries, and lamps are often found in old workings.

The immense number of ancient lamps which survive in museum and other collections – and which are constantly coming to light in excavations – can only be a small fraction of those once in use. That lamps were used in great quantities is illustrated by the 1600 lamps and fragments found in the large military camp at Vindonissa, near Basle, occupied for less than a century, from the time of Tiberius until about A.D.101.

Religious festivals and games were occasions on which the burning of lamps was customary. Caligula and Domitian lighted their gladiatorial shows and theatres with lamps, and thousands of lamps were lit during the celebrations of the Secular Games organised by the Emperor Philip I in A.D. 248. In the Greek theatre lamps were used to show that the action was set during the night. Their slapstick use in Comedy is indicated by a critical remark: 'It is vulgar to come on stage with a lamp and burn somebody'.

Street lighting, as a municipal responsibility, does not appear to have been introduced until the middle of the 5th century A.D., when Antioch was lit with tarred torches, but most Roman towns must have been brightly lit at night, in the commercial streets at least. Shops were lighted during the hours of darkness, when open, to show off their wares and to attract custom; lamps were placed on counters and over doors. At Pompeii several hundreds of such lamps were found in comparatively short lengths of street: the High Street to Stabiae had about 500 lamps in a stretch of 700 metres, and in Second Street, 132 shops had for illumination purposes some 396 lamps. Shrines at street corners were also illuminated at night, and many temples were brightly lit. Lamps were often lighted at graves and tombs, but as these were outside the town boundaries this would not help as far as street lighting was concerned, but would at least inform belated travellers of the proximity of a town.

Lamps were from early times an important item of temple furniture. From the famous Golden Lamp made by Callimachus and kept on the Athenian Acropolis to the ordinary clay example presented as a votive offering at many temples and shrines, the lamp is a common feature in the worship of the gods. In many places all over the ancient world, among them Sicily, Cyprus, Naukratis, and Athens, a variety of lamps with many nozzles, known collectively as 'sanctuary lamps', has been found. These were used from at least the 6th century B.C. down through Hellenistic times and during the Roman period. The Museum's collections include only fragmentary examples of the 6th and 5th centuries B.C., but dozens of lamps of this sort, and date, were found in a temple of Demeter at Akragas in Sicily. A Hellenistic example with hundreds of nozzles arranged in several tiers on a conical structure was recently found at the shrine of an unnamed nymph at Kafizin in Cyprus.

Lamps were given in great numbers as votive offerings at some temples. When space became restricted in the sanctuary, the earlier offerings were cleared out to make room for subsequent votives. As the offerings thus removed were still sacred they could not be thrown away, and so it often happened that pits were dug within the temple grounds, and they were buried. Sir Charles Newton found several such caches of lamps in the Temenos of Demeter at Cnidus during the British Museum excavations at that site in 1859.

The third main use for lamps in the ancient world – and probably the main source of modern collections – was their function as tomb furniture. This practice dates back to the 3rd millennium in the Levant, and was widespread during classical times in the Mediterranean area, although more prevalent in some places than others. Lamps placed in tombs were probably, like the pottery and glass, jewellery and other objects buried with them, merely the property of the dead person, but may have had some symbolic or religious purpose. Many seem to be unused: there is no sign of blackening around the wick-hole; these were probably purchased specially for funerary use, though they differ in no way from the domestic variety. Occasionally a lamp found in a tomb was not placed there as funerary furniture, but was left behind by a tomb robber, and can be considerably later in date than other objects left in the tomb.

Thus, in antiquity, lamps had, in the main, three purposes: domestic or commercial illumination, funerary function, and votive use. Exactly the same type of lamp could be employed for any of these reasons, and there would seem to be very little connection between the use to which a Roman lamp was put, and the decorative scene appearing on it.

Three methods of lamp manufacture were used – hand-modelling, throwing on the wheel, and moulding. Hand-modelled lamps were probably made at all periods; they are certainly as early as the end of the 7th century B.C., when examples were made in some quantity in Athens, but they were never very common, and wheel-made and moulded lamps were easier to produce. The hand-modelled example illustrated (pl. 4d) was found in a Hellenistic tomb near the acropolis of Sparta, and was dated by the excavator to the 2nd century B.C.

Wheel-made lamps were made throughout the period covered by this booklet, although from Hellenistic times onwards the moulded lamp was more popular with makers and users. The 'cocked-hat' type of lamp was formed by merely folding or pinching-in the edges of a shallow bowl or plate as soon as it had been thrown. A lamp with a bridged nozzle was thrown as a bowl, more or less open according to its type. When the clay had dried 'leather hard' it was placed upside down on the wheel, and the base turned with a metal or wooden tool. After this the nozzle, which had been previously fashioned by hand and allowed to dry somewhat, was luted on and the wick-hole cut through it and the shoulder. The handle, if any, was modelled and added in the same way. On many lamps of the 4th and 3rd centuries B.C. a lug was applied to the shoulder and pierced vertically. This lug would seem to be simply a means whereby the lamp could be hung up when not in use, by threading a piece of string through the hole. The lamp would then hang in such a position that any oil left in it would not spill. The lug is not usually found on lamps with handles. The pierced lug was rather a short-lived feature, but unpierced lugs, of no functional use, continued to be applied to or moulded with lamps for two or three hundred years. This decorative lug was occasionally modelled in the form of a dolphin.

Although hollow-moulding was used for terracottas in Greece at least as early as the mid-6th century, this process does not seem to have been used for lamps until the early 3rd century B.C. A patrix or model from which a mould could be taken was fashioned by hand from clay, or perhaps carved from wood. If clay it was fired as hard as possible. Moulds were taken from this by pressing on clay until a substantial layer covered one half (top or bottom) of the patrix. The clay was then allowed to dry somewhat (it must not be allowed to dry out too much or it will shrink and split on the patrix), and the other half made in the same way. When sufficiently dry, the halves of the mould were removed from the patrix.

Plaster moulds were used rather than clay examples in Roman times in most areas, and these were made in the same fashion, but there was no necessity to remove the mould from the patrix before it was thoroughly dry, as there is little or no shrinkage in plaster. Clay moulds need to be fired, but plaster does not. As many moulds as were thought necessary would be taken from the patrix. Lamp makers must have held a considerable stock of moulds: a lamp cannot be removed from a mould with ease or without damage until some little time has elapsed, putting the mould out of use for that period.

Plaster moulds must have worn out comparatively quickly, gradually disintegrating through repeated use; clay moulds lasted much longer and details did not blur as easily. Not many moulds have survived, although thousands must have been in use over a period of many hundred years. This perhaps indicates that most moulds were made of a perishable substance such as plaster (several plaster moulds have been found in Egypt), but the main, though not conclusive evidence for this is on the lamps produced from such moulds: air bubbles often form on the surface of a plaster mould when it is being made. When clay is pressed into such moulds the air bubbles are reproduced in reverse as raised globules. A high proportion of moulded Roman lamps have these globules.

When the clay mould has been fired or the plaster mould dried it is ready for use. Of the two possible methods of production one is more tedious and difficult than the other. In both methods wet clay is pressed into each half of the mould in a thin layer, and any excess trimmed away. In the more probable production method (evidence for which is provided by the occurrence of moulds bearing guide lines scratched on the edge, or by positioning bosses and hollows – pl. 16a, b, c), the top and bottom halves of a lamp were joined by pressing the two parts of the mould together, in register, with the moist clay pieces inside. When the pieces had dried sufficiently, the mould would be removed, and the requisite holes pierced: filling-hole, wick-hole, air-hole, handle-piercing. The joints would be made good with wet clay where necessary, and excess clay on the outside trimmed away. The other possible, but less likely, method was to allow the two halves to dry separately in the two pieces of the mould until they could be removed. The necessary holes would then be pierced in the upper half, and when dry enough the pieces luted together. The final stage in the actual fashioning of the lamp was the attachment of the handle, if this feature had not been formed in the mould with the lamp. The lamp was allowed to dry out thoroughly, treated with a glaze preparation, and then fired.

Clay, Glazes and Firing

Suitable potting clay was available in many places all over the Mediterranean world, but it differs in composition from district to district. This means that the fabric of lamps from one particular area has a different appearance from that of similarly shaped products made elsewhere. The texture and colour, the presence or absence of grits and mica specks, the appearance of any glazed decoration all help to assign a lamp to its place of origin. Unfortunately, with many fabrics, there is a great deal more work to be done on this subject – the identification of the place of manufacture – before it will be possible to say with any certainty that a particular piece comes from a particular site. The problem is further complicated by the differences in colour and texture brought about by variations in firing conditions and temperatures, and in clay constituents, even from one small area.

Glazes differed in place and time as much as the clay body. The main purpose of a glaze is to render the lamp less permeable to the fuel it contains, and its decorative function is only secondary. This did not, of course, prevent a lamp maker applying his glaze in such a manner as to give a pleasing appearance to his products. Most ancient glazes are not true glazes since they are not vitreous, but a slip or thin wash of clay which owes its colour to the presence of iron oxides and to the conditions of firing (as does the colour of the clay body itself). If a suspension in water is made of clay which has a good proportion of iron oxide— in many cases the potting clay itself has sufficient oxide—and to this slip is added a peptizing agent, such as potash, to keep the minute particles of clay from coagulating, the resulting solution, when applied to a lamp, will produce a glaze when fired, the colour depending on the firing technique.

Thus, to produce a red glaze, the treated lamp is fired in a clear, oxidising atmosphere. A black glaze is brought about by a smoky, reducing atmosphere within the kiln, caused by the introduction of damp fuel and by stopping air entering the firing chamber. This treatment also turns the unglazed parts black or grey. To produce a lamp with a pink or buff body decorated with black glaze a three-stage firing is necessary: first the lamp is fired in an oxidising (smokeless) atmosphere, the main function of which is to bake the object; if taken from the kiln at this point a buff or pink body with a sintered red or brown glaze is the result. Most Roman lamps went through this stage only. After this, damp fuel is introduced to the kiln and all entry for air blocked up. The damp atmosphere, and the incomplete combustion of the fuel producing carbon monoxide, result in a change of colour: the body turns grey and the sintered glaze black. The third stage consists of the reintroduction of dry fuel and air to the firing chamber. The oxidising flame so generated reverses the effect of the reducing atmosphere of the preceding stage as far as the clay body and the unglazed parts of the lamp are concerned; they return to the buff or pink colour produced by the first stage. But the glaze is not affected by this third state – it remains the black colour obtained in the second firing stage. The three stages follow one upon the other in one continuous firing, and the kiln is not cooled or unloaded between stages.

The three main methods of applying the glaze slip were by painting, dipping, and pouring, or a combination of these. The bands of glaze which decorate many Greek lamps were painted on as the lamp turned on the wheel; the interiors were often glazed by pouring in slip, swilling it round and pouring the surplus out. Roman lamps were usually glazed by dipping the whole lamp quickly into the glaze medium, or by pouring the slip over the lamp. Finger marks, showing where the lamp was held during this process, are often found.

Many pottery objects, lamps amongst them, of Roman date were coated with true vitreous glazes, although they are vastly outnumbered by wares decorated with the sintered metallic slip described above. Lead glaze wares, usually of a green colour, were produced at many sites mainly in the first three centuries A.D. – Tarsus and other places in Asia Minor, South Russia, Egypt and Italy, at St. Remy-en-Rollat in France, Cologne in Germany (pl. C), and also Holt in Denbighshire, and Colchester. This kind of glaze required two separate firings; the unglazed lamp was fired and when cool the lead glaze mixture was applied to the biscuit body. A subsequent firing in a muffle kiln fused the glaze dressing into a vitreous coating.

The usual type of kiln used in antiquity was the vertical variety. This had, normally, a circular fuel chamber with a combined flue and stoke-hole at one side. Above this was the firing-floor, pierced in many places to allow the hot air and gases to enter the firing chamber. This chamber was domed, with a vent at the top: it was built from clay for each firing and broken down to retrieve the finished products. Before the dome was completed the lamps were stacked tightly on the firing floor within the kiln, resting one upon the other. Occasionally horizontal through-draught kilns were used. The firing temperatures probably varied from place to place and with each firing, but in the main would seem to have been a little under 1000°C. The fuel used was in most cases wood, and the firing probably took at least 24 hours and perhaps twice as long, with a slow build up of temperature and a gradual cooling. Sometimes accidents happened and the heat got out of hand and excessive, resulting in warped lamps, often fused together, the fabric very hard and discoloured. The examples shown on pl. 16d, e are from kilns at Ephesus, and are probably those described by Wood (the discoverer and excavator of the site of the Temple of the Ephesian Artemis) as being found dumped inside a tower of the city wall: 'We came across a great quantity of pottery, consisting chiefly of lamps, some of which were joined together, having been spoilt in the baking'.*

*J. T. Wood, *Discoveries at Ephesus*, London, 1877, p.79.

Colour plate A

Colour plate B

Oil lamps have been used in Europe from remote antiquity, some stone examples being found in Paleolithic contexts. In the Mediterranean area, sherds used as lamps appear in Palestine before 2000 B.C., followed shortly by 'cocked-hat' lamps. Minoan lamps, of sauce-boat shape with wide unbridged nozzles (pl. 1a), were produced somewhat later in Crete. A few lamps have been found on Mycenaean sites (pl. 1b), but they do not seem to be particularly popular as a means of lighting; torches were probably preferred, and there is only one disputed reference to a lamp in Homer's works. The use of lamps in the Greek world appears to cease during the dark ages after the fall of the Mycenaean palaces, although a lipped bowl from a late protogeometric tomb at Mycenae has been described tentatively as a lamp. Pottery lamps were, however, employed continuously in the Palestine area. An excellent 'cocked-hat' lamp from Hazor, of Late Bronze Age date, has recently been acquired by the Museum. This type of lamp has never died out: they are still made in Malta, Corsica and Sicily. The first Athenian lamps (early 7th century B.C.) are of 'cocked-hat' form, and probably owe their origin ultimately to eastern influence. The Punic version of the 'cocked-hat' lamp – usually with two wick-rests (pl. 1d) – flourished from the 7th to at least the 3rd century B.C., while in Cyprus examples with single wick-rests (pl. 1c) are as early as the Cypro-Geometric period (*circa* 950-850 B.C.) and remain in use until Ptolemaic times. 'Cocked-hat' lamps were found with Athenian wheelmade lamps in warehouses at Al Mina in Syria, dating between 430 and 375 B.C.

Some of the earliest lamps with bridged nozzles were produced in Asia Minor, during the latter part of the 7th century B.C. (pl. 3a), this feature apparently being a Greek invention (or more accurately, a re-invention: in the Department of Western Asiatic Antiquities is a large stone multiple lamp with bridged nozzles, from Atchana in Syria, and dating to about 1600 B.C.). Once the value of this obviously more efficient type of nozzle was recognized it was copied all over the Greek world, although the unbridged nozzle did not die out quickly.

During the 6th, 5th and 4th centuries B.C., and probably somewhat later, Athens appears to be the major producer of new types, and these high-quality lamps were exported all over the Mediterranean and Black Sea, together with the luxury Attic vases much desired in many countries. Athenian lamps are often so superior in workmanship to the products of other localities, that we need not search for any other reason for their importation. The shapes and styles were copied by local potters, with some occasional success, but very few can compare with the best Attic products. But Athens itself imported foreign lamps on a small scale, mainly from Asia Minor, from the 7th century B.C. onwards.

The general trend in design was for the body to become less open and shallow, and the nozzle to lengthen. Glaze, which at first had been used purely functionally to lessen porosity began to be applied artistically as well. Lamps were, on the whole, down to the 3rd century, strictly utilitarian objects, with nothing frivolous about them. This was mainly determined by their method of manufacture and the limits set by the potter's wheel. The next technical step was the introduction of the moulded lamp, with its greater opportunities for new shapes, mass production, and decorative design. This occurred about the beginning of the 3rd century B.C. in the Greek world, and was thenceforward the principal means of manufacture, although wheel-made lamps continued to be made. The first moulded lamps were very similar in appearance to the contemporary wheel-made examples. A moulded lamp from Cyprus (pl. 4c) is quite early – about the end of the 3rd century, and shows how quickly relief figure decoration began to be used after it became technically possible. In the 3rd century also, the first lamps modelled in the shape of human heads were produced. These and other plastic forms were popular products for many hundreds of years (pls. 6f, 9a, b, d).

During the Hellenistic period the moulding of lamps spread to most parts of the Mediterranean, although the main areas of production were in the eastern half. Many lamps were exported from western Asia Minor in the last two centuries B.C. Lamps of the type shown on pl. 5b, c have been found on a great many sites in the east end of the Mediterranean. They were certainly made in Asia Minor, probably at Ephesus, where moulds have been found (pl. 16a).

Another Asia Minor type of similar date, which is found in many places is that shown on pls. 4e and 5a. It is not certain where lamps of this kind were made, but hundreds were found in votive deposits at Cnidus, so it is probable that they were produced in the neighbourhood. This type is wheel-made, and is often decorated with appliqué patterns or separately moulded designs.

In the west, during the last two centuries B.C. lamps somewhat similar to the eastern Hellenistic moulded lamps were made, leading on the Italian products of Late Republican date (pl. 6e, f). During the late first century B.C. and the early 1st century A.D., the new Italian shapes (pl. 7) swamped the market, were exported everywhere, and were copied by provincial workshops. These lamps, with their voluted nozzles, both round and angular (the nozzle volute probably evolved in Asia Minor), and allowing the employment of a large area for decorative relief pictures, were, at their best, among the finest mould-made lamps ever produced. This was during the first half of the 1st century; the shapes went on later, into the 2nd century at some factories, but the lamps produced were much coarser in style and technique. A type of lamp basically similar to the round-nozzle voluted lamps, but often much larger, with two or more nozzles and with a decorative attachment over the handle, was produced contemporaneously with these (pl. 8a, b, c). This attachment is often triangular, with a relief design, but can occasionally be leaf-shaped, or in the form of a crescent. The examples illustrated are Italian, Cnidian, and British, showing the wide distribution of the shape. During this time, wheel-made lamps like pl. 6a were being produced and are found in some numbers in Greece and Sicily.

In the 1st century A.D., and to a lesser degree later on, lamps made in Italy were exported all over the Roman world, and beyond. Although in the early Imperial period official policy to a certain extent protected Italian industrial undertakings, economic and political factors soon ensured that the Italian domination of the market was comparatively short-lived; local lamp makers everywhere copied the Italian shapes, either directly by using an imported lamp as a patrix to produce a mould, or indirectly by using them as a pattern to be imitated. Except perhaps to a limited extent in North Africa, the large scale export of lamps from central and southern Italy was over by the beginning of the 2nd century A.D.

About the middle of the 1st century A.D. a new shape was introduced, again apparently with its origin in Italy. Examples of the fat type (pl. 10b) have been found at Herculaneum, proving their existence before A.D. 79, and smaller lamps, similar to pl. 10a, were produced in their thousands by Italian workshops during the last years of the 1st century, and well into the 2nd century. Many of them have three-part maker's names (see below p. 24). This shape of lamp was so simple and practical that it was copied in every part of the Mediterranean world, and in other places subservient to Roman rule. The basic shape was in use until at least the 4th century A.D. and probably later. In Italy itself the shape modifies: it is not quite so crisp as time goes on, the handle becomes squatter and coarser, the rim is often decorated with floral designs, and the nozzle is less well-defined. The glaze gets less good in quality, and decorative details are often blurred and worn (pl. 11d).

The great influence of this shape of lamp is shown by the wide distribution of lamps ultimately based upon it: 1st and 2nd century lamps from Asia Minor (pls. 10c, 11a, b, c); 2nd and 3rd century lamps from Egypt, Cyprus and Tarsus (pl. 12a-f); lamps from North Africa (pl. 11f); also those lamps which are undoubtedly the finest products of the lamp maker's art, the lamps made in Corinth and Athens during the 2nd and 3rd centuries A.D. (pl. 13a, b), and their debased descendants and copies of the 3rd and later centuries (pl. 13c-f).

About the middle of the second half of the 1st century A.D. a new type of lamp was produced, apparently in North Italy (pl. 10d, e, f). It is one of the few pottery shapes which may have been copied from bronze originals. These so-called 'factory lamps' were made in thousands and ousted to a great extent the lamps of central and southern Italy from the markets of the north-west provinces. They were not popular in the east and south of the Empire. Lamps of this type were found at Pompeii, and therefore antedate the destruction in A.D. 79, but not by much, as the specimens found were in crates, evidently just received from the makers, and not yet unpacked for sale. The finest examples were produced in the last quarter of the 1st century. Degeneration thereafter sets in, and by the end of the 2nd century the type is much debased. By this time, the original Italian workshops have ceased to be the main centres of production, lamp makers in Germany, France, and Britain all manufacturing their own poor copies (pl. 10g, h). The type continued to be made well into the 3rd century; examples of this date were found recently in a Mithraeum at Caernarvon. The green-glazed helmet lamp (pl. C), made at Cologne about A.D. 200 is based upon the factory lamp, and so is the fine Italian example on the same plate, which is about a hundred years earlier. Most Italian examples have no handle, while the majority of the provincial lamps of this type are furnished with this feature.

After the 3rd century A.D. very few lamps were made in the north-west provinces; perhaps oil became an expensive luxury, but in Greece, Asia Minor, the Levant and North Africa, pottery lamps never ceased being produced. The 4th and later centuries were not noted for the quality of their lamps, many poor examples being made in some parts of the Empire, the Italian lamp shown on pl. 14c, for instance, and the oval Cypriote lamp next to it. In 5th century Palestine, the so-called 'candlestick' lamp (pl. 14a) was produced – the branched decoration near the wick-hole apparently originated from a representation of the *menorah* or many-branched candlestick. It was the forerunner of a shape which, in the Islamic east Mediterranean, lasted for a millennium.

In Egypt, during the 3rd and 4th centuries A.D., a popular lamp was that now known as a frog lamp (pl. 14d). It was made in vast numbers, probably in Upper Egypt. Some of the finest have a frog in relief on the upper side, but in most cases the frog design has disintegrated and only parts of the animal, such as the back legs, appear. Palm branches and rosettes also decorate this type of lamp. A frog lamp has recently been found at Athens. In cases like this, the odd, isolated lamp found far from its source may be a personal import, brought into a country in antiquity by its owner who purchased it elsewhere, and does not necessarily indicate a trade connection. Similarly, a Syrian lamp found at Vindonissa, in Switzerland, is probably an example of this.

Perhaps in the 4th century, but certainly in the 5th and 6th centuries A.D., the 'African' lamp appears, often with Christian designs: the Cross, the Sacred Monogram, saints, and Biblical scenes. The type is very attractive (pl. D), and is usually in a brick-red clay. It has been said that it was first evolved in Cyrenaica; its manufacture spread to other parts of North Africa, and to Greece. Those found in Italy were probably imported, but Sicily produced its own version, rather debased, and in a buff-coloured clay (pl. 12i). One or two of African origin are said to have been found in London, but adequate details of provenience are lacking. The chronology of the 'African' lamp and its copies has not been established with any certainty. The same may be said about many late lamps, such as pl. 14f; examples of this type have been found in Christian catacombs in Rome. The circular lamp (pl. 14e) is also a puzzle as far as dating is concerned. Some have been found at Antioch-on-the-Orontes, and basically similar lamps have been excavated at Corinth and Sicily. A tentative date would put this type in the 6th century A.D.

In the 5th, 6th, and 7th centuries some very well-made lamps were produced in Western Asia Minor (pl. 15a-d). The majority of this type in the Museum's collections were found at Ephesus and Calymnos. Other places from which examples have come include Smyrna, Miletus, Sardis, and as far afield as Corinth in Greece. Many bear an impressed foot-print stamp underneath, reminiscent of those found on some 1st century Italian lamps. It is interesting to see, at this late date, pagan scenes represented on these lamps, side by side with examples carrying Christian symbols. The latest lamp illustrated (pl. 15e) bears the name of an Egyptian bishop; it was made in Upper Egypt in the 7th or 8th century A.D.

The story of pottery lamps does not, of course, end here, although by this date their manufacture had ceased in many places in Dark Age Europe. This was no doubt due to the lack of oil in large quantities: in countries where oil-bearing plants grow readily, pottery lamps continued to be made until the present day.

Decorative Features

Early lamps were, on the whole, undecorated, but very soon glaze began to be used decoratively, although its utilitarian function was never subordinated. Most decorative features on classical Greek lamps were dictated by the limitations of the wheel: bands of glaze, or concentric ridges, produced as the lamp was turned, usually with aesthetically satisfying results. Only occasionally are other methods met with, as on a 5th century lamp found at Camarina in Sicily, which has several impressed palmettes on the shoulder, made with a stamp.

With the introduction of moulding as a manufacturing process, new shapes, and a very much extended range of relief decoration were possible. However, on the wide and sloping shoulders of most Hellenistic lamps only a limited variety of designs could be used. These were mainly of a linear or floral character, figures (as pl. 4c) being seldom used, the space available being unsuitable for elaborate scenes. An interesting variation combining wheel-made lamps and moulded decoration is often seen on lamps of the same type as that shown on pl. 4e. To the wheel-made body were applied separately-moulded decorative features, such as representations of theatrical masks.

The first lamps to make the whole of the upper surface of the body available for relief decoration were produced in Italy during late Republican times (pl. 6e). These still have a Hellenistic shape, but in the early Imperial period, at the end of the last century B.C., the first examples of the eventually almost universally popular Roman relief lamps were designed and manufactured.

The concave upper surface (known as the discus) of these lamps allowed a large area to be used for decorative purposes, and in which it was easy to fit an adequate and complete vignette, and many Roman lamps, of various forms, and ranging in date until about the 6th century A.D. have, as their main feature, a decorated discus of this kind. The scenes used are many and varied, and include religious and mythological themes, representations of aspects of daily life, the circus and theatre, animals, inanimate objects, and floral designs.

The Olympian deities, and other gods and personifications appear on many lamps, in various typical attitudes and dress. Zeus with his eagle and thunderbolt, Apollo playing the lyre, Artemis hunting, Hermes carrying his herald's staff, Serapis with a corn measure on his head, Selene and Helios, with the moon's crescent and the sun's rays respectively, Eros in a great variety of scenes, Victory and Fortuna with their attributes; these are but a few of such representations. Lamps showing sacrifices and the pouring of libations are also found. Some of the designs were taken from famous masterpieces of statuary no longer extant (pl. 12e). Mythological subjects include many examples showing Herakles engaged in his labours and adventures. Also depicted, to mention just a few random scenes, are Odysseus, Perseus, Actaeon attacked by his hounds, Leda and the Swan, satyrs and maenads, and Aeneas escaping from Troy.

Shepherds and fishermen, horsemen and hunters, the milling of grain and the fetching of water, washing and cleansing, board-games and bedroom scenes, are all aspects of daily life which appear on lamps. Among the most favoured features of entertainment in Roman times were chariot races and gladiatorial combats, and these are represented on a great many lamps. Actors performing, and the many examples of masks on lamps reflect the popularity of the play, and other entertainments illustrated include jugglers, performing animals, boxers and tightrope walkers.

Animals, usually shown singly, but sometimes in groups, such as hounds attacking deer, are found on a great many relief lamps. Domestic and wild animals, birds, fish, shellfish, and insects are all represented. Small objects like anchors, drinking cups, mixing bowls, wine amphorae, horns of plenty, and altars, and larger things – buildings and boats, for example – were also popular items in the decoration of lamps, while many are found with linear and geometric decorations, and others have rosettes, wreaths and palm branches.

Basically, the decorative aspects of late antique lamps are determined by the type and shape, and differ little from the earlier Roman relief lamps: human figures, animals, inanimate objects, and linear and floral designs. The scenic aspects are normally simpler and the decorative elements more profuse. The Cross appears towards the end of the 3rd century on lamps made in Egypt, and becomes progressively more frequent.

Many Roman lamps were glazed, even if rather poorly in some cases, but except for its colouring properties, the use of glaze was not decorative. At the end of the 1st century and in the 2nd century A.D. in Britain, however, a superficial decorative technique was often used which had no useful purpose, except to make the lamp more attractive. Like many Romano-British pots, before firing the whole surface was dusted with particles of mica, which form a scintillating golden or silver-coloured coating, dense or speckled, depending on the amount of mica used.

Inscriptions

Many lamps have inscriptions of some kind on them; their presence is due, in the main, to one of three reasons: the maker's name or mark, the owner's name or mark, or a votive dedication.

Maker's names, a form of trade mark and advertisement, do not seem to antedate the Hellenistic period, and only become common in the 1st century B.C., both in Italy and the Greek lands. They can be produced by incision, cut directly into the unfired lamp; scratched in reverse in the mould, producing moulded relief letters; or perhaps incised on the patrix, the result in this case being a moulded sunk inscription. Lettering formed by the use of a stamp was common in the Roman period. Footprint-shaped stamps were very popular. Although in some cases the stamp may have been pressed directly into the lamp, it seems doubtful whether the clay would be moist enough to receive a satisfactory impression when it was dry enough to be removed from the mould and handled. The majority of lamps with stamped inscriptions received these from the moulds in which they were fashioned. Clay moulds could be stamped directly, resulting in relief letters, or the patrix could be stamped, producing relief letters in the mould and hollow letters on the lamp; this must have been the case with plaster moulds.

Maker's names, in conjunction with the fabric of their products, can be a considerable help in tracing the country of origin of lamps. The situation is confused somewhat by the large scale export of lamps, but a manufacturing centre can often be confirmed by the presence of a signature. For example, the great majority of lamps signed with abbreviated three-part names, such as C OPPI RES, C COR VRS, L FABR MASC, and L M ADIEC, can be regarded as of Italian origin, and most of them seem to date from the end of the 1st century A.D. and well into the 2nd century. Exceptions here are lamps bearing the signatures L CAE SAE and C IVN BIT, which are perhaps a hundred years later in date.

The Italian factory lamps, when signed, usually employ only the *cognomen* in full: FORTIS, IEGIDI, STROBILI, EVCARPI, and many more, and in nearly every case the inscription is in relief; very few lamps of other types have maker's names in raised letters.

Some signatures which denote place or origin are: HOSCRI – France, SER – Germany, PVLLAENI – North Africa, ΛΟΥΚΙΟΥ – Corinth, ΕΛΠΙΔΗΦΟΡΟΥ – Athens, ΠΡΟΚΑΓΥΡ – Sicily, ΚΕΡΔΩΝ – Egypt, ΣΦΥΡΙΔΩΝΟΣ – Cyprus. A few lamp-makers seem to have had branches in other countries. Lamps with the name PHOETASPI were made both in North Italy and in Egypt; ROMANESIS, whose factory was probably in the neighbourhood of Cnidus in Asia Minor, and who exported much of his wares, may have had another workshop in Dalmatia, unless (and this is more likely) the large numbers of lamps with his name found these were imports. FAVSTI, an Egyptian lampmaker's signature, appears also on lamps made at Petra.

Another source of confusion can arise when the practice, common in some countries, of using an imported lamp as a patrix produces, for example, lamps of provincial origin with an Italian maker's name – a lamp from a tomb at Curium, signed C OPPI RES, but made in Cyprus, is in the Museum's collections.

Although not often found, exhortations by the potter to the public to buy were occasionally scratched on a lamp before firing. The ship-form lamp (pl. 9d) has "take me, the Helioserapis" incised underneath. This is somewhat obscure, but it has been suggested that a 'helioserapis' was the name of a type of lamp, just as some modern light bulbs bear the names of ancient deities. A related example is on a lamp made at Petra (pl. 7j) where the maker's name is written in a cursive Nabataean script together with the word "Peace" or "Hail".

Owner's names or marks are comparatively rare and occur mainly on Greek lamps, where an initial or two might be scratched on the object to denote possession. As this was done after

Colour plate C

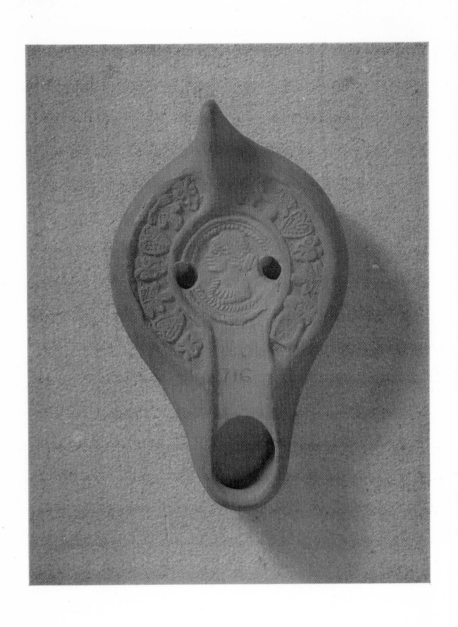

Colour plate D

purchase, the scratching was made after firing, and often through the glaze. An unusual example of what appears to be an owner's inscription was incised underneath a lamp (pl. 4a) *before* firing; a free translation reads "I belong to the most lecherous Pausanias".

Lamps formed a large proportion of the votive offerings at certain shrines, and occasionally inscriptions were cut into them by the votaries. A fragment of a lamp in the Museum, found at Naukratis in Egypt, is devoted to the Dioscuri – the Heavenly Twins. Related to this kind of inscription is that upon a 6th century Greek lamp in the Hermitage Museum at Leningrad, which bears the words "I am a lamp and I shine for gods and men". A similar usage is that found on some lamps from Samothrace, where letters scratched upon them seem to indicate that they were reserved for the use of initiates taking part in a mystery cult.

In the Levant and in Egypt, dedications to Christian saints and abbots appear on lamps. These inscriptions were moulded with the lamps, which would appear to be either votives or souvenirs of a pilgrimage, purchased at a shrine. The example on pl. 15e bears a request for "the intercession of the Holy Bishop Abba Joseph".

Texts such as OB CIVES SERVATOS ("for saving the citizens") often appear on 1st century Italian lamps (and their provincial copies) bearing the figure of Victory (pl. 7g). Similarly, other lamps showing Victory have one or another variant of ANNVM NOVVM FAVSTVM FELICEM ("a happy and prosperous New Year") on her shield. Very rarely, the characters depicted on picture lamps are named. Virgil's Tityrus the shepherd is shown on one lamp (pl. 7i) with his name behind him, while Diogenes, in a large pottery jar, is named on a fragmentary lamp. Other inscriptions name rival gladiators: ACVVIVS V HERMEROS S, and on an amusing lamp showing cupids playing with the club and cup of Herakles, one of a group trying to lift the club shouts ADIVATE SODALES – "help, comrades!".

Short Bibliography

GENERAL

R. J. Forbes, *Studies in Ancient Technology*, Vol. VI, Leiden, 1958.

F. Fremersdorf, *Römische Bildlampen*, Bonn, 1922.

F. W. Robins, *The Story of the Lamp*, London, 1939.

MUSEUM CATALOGUES, ETC.

D. M. Bailey, *Lamps in the Victoria and Albert Museum (Opuscula Atheniensia VI)*, Lund, 1965.

M. L. Bernhard, *Lampki Starożytne*, Warsaw, 1955. (This contains a very full bibliography).

J. Brants, *Antieke Terra-cotta Lampen*, Leiden, 1913.

J. Deneauve, *Lampes de Carthage*, Paris, 1969.

M. A. Evelein, *De Romeinsche Lampen*, 'S-Gravenhage, 1928.

R. Haken, *Roman Lamps in the Prague National Museum*, Prague, 1958.

G. Heres, *Die punischen und griechischen Tonlampen der staatlichen Museen zu Berlin*, 1969.

C. Iconomu, *Opaite Greco-Romane*, Dobregea, 1968.

D. Iványi, *Die pannonischen Lampen*, Budapest, 1935.

L. Lerat, *Les Lampes Antiques*, Besançon, 1954.

H. Menzel, *Antike Lampen im Römisch-Germanischen Zentralmuseum*, Mainz, 1954.

M. Ponsich, *Les Lampes Romaines en Terre Cuite de la Maurétanie Tingitane*, Rabat, 1961.

T. Szentléleky, *Ancient Lamps [in Hungary]*. Amsterdam, 1969.

O. Waldhauer, *Die antiken Tonlampen*, St Petersburg, 1914.

H. B. Walters, *Catalogue of the Greek and Roman lamps in the British Museum*, London, 1914.

EXCAVATION REPORTS

P. V. C. Baur, *Excavations at Dura-Europos, Final Report IV, Part III, The Lamps*, Yale, 1947.

A. Bovon, *Lampes d'Argos*, Paris, 1966.

O. Broneer, *Corinth, Vol. IV, Part II, Terracotta Lamps*, Harvard, 1930.

P. Bruneau, *Delos XXVI, Les Lampes*, Paris, 1965.

H. Deringer, *Römische Lampen aus Lauriacum*, Linz, 1965.

H. Goldman, *Excavations at Gözlü Kule, Tarsus, Vol. I*, Princeton, 1950.

C. Grandjouan, *The Athenian Agora, Vol. VI, Terracottas and Plastic Lamps of the Roman Period*, Princeton, 1961.

R. H. Howland, *The Athenian Agora, Vol. IV, Greek Lamps and their Survivals*, Princeton, 1958.

S. Loeschcke, *Lampen aus Vindonissa*, Zurich, 1919.

F. Miltner, *Forschungen in Ephesos*, Band *IV*, *Heft* 2, Vienna,
1937.

J. Perlzweig, *The Athenian Agora*, Vol. *VII, Lamps of the Roman
Period*, Princeton, 1961.

W. M. F. Petrie, *Roman Ehnasya*, London, 1905.

M. Vegas, *Die römische Lampen von Neuss* (*Novaesium II*),
Berlin, 1966.

F. O. Waagé in *Antioch-on-the Orontes, Vols. I and III*, Princeton,
1934 and 1941.

A wealth of relevant material is also buried in a great number of
defunct and current periodical publications and journals dealing
with classical and near-eastern studies. Useful references to these
are supplied in the annual *Archäologische Bibliographie* published
with the *Jahrbuch des Deutschen Archäologischen Instituts*, and
in *Fasti Archaeologici*.

Unless otherwise indicated all lamps are in the Department of
Greek and Roman Antiquities.

Plate 1
(a) Lamp 130. Middle Minoan lamp from Palaikastro, Crete.
Circa 1700–1450 B.C.
(b) Lamp 97 4-1 1283. Mycenaean lamp from a tomb at
Enkomi in Cyprus. 1400-1200 B.C.
(c) Lamp 1960 3-2 1. Cypriote cocked-hat lamp from a tomb
at Amathus. *Circa* 6th century B.C.
(d) Lamp 1924 11-14 1. Punic cocked-hat lamp, said to be
from Malaga in Spain. 5th-4th century B.C. (Western
Asiatic Department).

Plate 2
Lamp 137. Lamp with three nozzles, held by a terracotta
figure of a woman. Made in Rhodes and found at Camirus.
About 600 B.C.

Plate 3
(a) Lamp 196. Found in the Archaic Temple of Artemis at
Ephesus, and made in Western Asia Minor.
End of the 7th century B.C.
(b) Lamp 65 7-20 24 (9). Toy lamp. Probably made at Athens.
5th century B.C.
(c) Lamp 174. Made at Athens between the last quarter of
the 6th century and *circa* 480 B.C.
(d) Lamp 1482. Made at Athens. Found at Gela in Sicily.
Second or third quarter of the 5th century B.C.
(e) Lamp 1962 9-20 1. Sicilian lamp, said to be from Sardinia.
5th–4th century B.C.
(f) Lamp 1959 7-12 1. Made at Corinth. Last quarter of the
5th century B.C.

Plate 4
(a) Lamp 230. Sicilian lamp, found at Gela. 4th century B.C.
(b) Lamp 64 10-7 1779. Made in Rhodes, found at Camirus.
Second half of 3rd century B.C.
(c) Lamp 302. Found at Kition in Cyprus. Second half of
3rd century B.C.
(d) Lamp 1923 2-12 343. Hand-modelled lamp from a
Hellenistic tomb at Sparta. 2nd century B.C.
(e) Lamp 366. Found in the Temenos of Demeter at Cnidus,
and perhaps made locally. Second half of the 2nd into
first quarter of the 1st century B.C.

Plate 5
(a) Lamp 388. Same site and same date as pl. 4e above.

(b) Lamp 333. Found at Ephesus, and probably made there between the last quarter of the 2nd century B.C. and the first quarter of the 1st century A.D.

(c) Lamp 330. As pl. 5b above.

Plate 6

(a) Lamp 63 7-28 233. Found at Akragas. Late 1st century B.C. into 1st century A.D.

(b) Lamp 1936 11-18 1. 'Pitcher lamp'. Made and found in Lower Egypt, probably at Alexandria. *Circa* 2nd century B.C.

(c) Lamp 267. 'Herodian' type. Said to be from Siloam; made in Palestine, *circa* 50 B.C.-A.D. 50

(d) Lamp WT 459. Made in Italy. Early 1st century A.D.

(e) Lamp 525. Altar and dolphins. Made in Italy towards the end of the 1st century B.C.

(f) Lamp 410. Late Republican. Made in Italy. 1st century B.C.

Plate 7

(a) Lamp 1962 8-29 1. Scallop shell. Made in Italy. Early 1st century A.D.

(b) Lamp 617. Eros. Made in Italy. Said to be from Naples. Middle years of the 1st century A.D.

(c) Lamp WT 490. Satyr and nymph. Made in Italy. Early 1st century A.D.

(d) Lamp 1925 11-20 33. Man and Horse. Made in Egypt in the first half of the 1st century A.D.

(e) Lamp 1949 10-11 52. Victory. Made in Germany. Found at Cologne. 1st century A.D.

(f) Lamp 554. Gladiators. Found in London, perhaps made in Britain. 1st century A.D. (Prehistoric and Romano-British Department).

(g) Lamp 652. Victory. Made in Italy. First half of the 1st century A.D.

(h) Lamp 768. Made in Italy. First half of the 1st century A.D.

(i) Lamp 661. The shepherd Tityrus, and sheep. Made in Italy. First half of the 1st century A.D.

(j) Lamp 1925 10-14 4. Scallop shell. Made and found at Petra. 1st century A.D., perhaps a little later.

(k) Lamp 709. Bird on bough. Found at Curium. Made in Cyprus. 1st century A.D.

Plate 8

(a) Lamp WT 466. Made in Italy. Late 1st century B.C. into early 1st century A.D.

(b) Lamp 846. From the Temenos of Demeter at Cnidus, and made locally. 1st century A.D.

(c) Lamp 940. Found in London. Probably made in Britain. 1st century A.D. (Prehistoric and Romano-British Department).

(d) Lamp 1955 7-16 1. Large four-nozzle lamp. Made in western Asia Minor, acquired in Smyrna. Signed *ΔΙΟΝΥΣΙΟΥ*. 1st century A.D.

(e) Lamp 443. Multiple lamp. Made in Italy. Signed LCAMSA. Last years of 1st century A.D.

Plate 9

(a) Lamp 1945 11-29 1. Bull's head. Made in Italy. First half of 1st century A.D.

(b) Lamp 56 9-2 32. Grotesque face. Perhaps made at Athens, and found at Mytilene. 2nd century B.C.

(c) Lamp WT 421. 'Bird Head' lamp. Made in Italy. Second half of 1st century A.D.

(d) Lamp 390. Ship form. Made at Cnidus. Found in the sea off Pozzuoli in Italy. 1st century A.D., perhaps the second half.

Plate 10

(a) Lamp 1007. Drinking cup. Made in Italy. Signed CIVNDRAC. First half of 2nd century A.D.

(b) Lamp 1048. Zeus and his eagle. Made in Italy in the middle years of the 1st century A.D.

(c) Lamp 68 6-20 198. Made at Ephesus, where it was found. Last years of the 1st century A.D.

(d) Lamp 907. Factory lamp. Made in Italy. Signed FONTEIVS. Last quarter of the 1st century A.D.

(e) Lamp 889. Factory lamp. Made in Italy. Signed IEGIDI. About 100 A.D.

(f) Lamp 896. Factory lamp, short form. Made in Italy. Signed CDESSI. About 100 A.D.

(g) Lamp 1949 10-11 49. Factory lamp. Made in Germany, found at Cologne. Second half of 2nd century A.D.

(h) Lamp 935. Factory lamp. Made in Britain, found in London. 2nd century A.D. (Prehistoric and Romano-British Department).

Plate 11

(a) Lamp 1246. Made at Cnidus, where it was found. Signed ROMANESIS. Second half of 1st century A.D.

(b) Lamp 1293. Gladiators. From the Temenos of Demeter at Cnidus, and made locally. Signed ROMANESIS. First half of 2nd century A.D.

(c) Lamp 1239. Horse. From Cnidus, where it was made. 2nd century A.D.

(d) Lamp 1962 8-29 2. Crater. Made in Italy about the turn of the 2nd and 3rd centuries A.D. Signed AMACHI.

(e) Lamp 626. Circus scene. Made in Italy. Signed SAECVL. Probably first half of 3rd century A.D.

(f) Lamp 57 12-18 178. Found at Carthage; made locally. Probably 3rd century A.D.

Plate 12   **31**

(a) Lamp 1925 11-20 29. Europa and the Bull. Made in Egypt, probably Alexandria. 3rd century A.D.

(b) Lamp 1925 11-20 41. Eros in goat chariot. Made in Egypt. 3rd century A.D.

(c) Lamp EC 825. Cross. Made in Egypt. End of 3rd century, perhaps into the 4th century A.D. (Department of Medieval and Later Antiquities).

(d) Lamp 1311. Wreath. Made at Tarsus, where it was found. 2nd century A.D.

(e) Lamp 1289. Athena and Poseidon – the central figures of the West Pediment of the Parthenon. Found at Salamis; probably made in Cyprus. 3rd century A.D.

(f) Lamp 1202. Hound and deer. Made in Egypt. Said to be from London. 2nd century A.D. (Prehistoric and Romano-British Department).

(g) Lamp 477. Made in Italy. Last years of the 1st century A.D., into the 2nd century. Signed MNOVIVSTI.

(h) Lamp 504. Made in Egypt and found at Naukratis. 1st century B.C.

(i) Lamp OA 300. Early Christian, made in Sicily. About 7th century A.D. (Department of Medieval and Later Antiquities).

Plate 13

(a) Lamp 1920 5-12 1. Athena. Made at Corinth. From Athens. Signed ΛΟΥΚΙΟΥ. 2nd century A.D.

(b) Lamp 1204. Zeus. From Athens. Signed ΠΡΕΙΜΟΥ. Early 3rd century A.D.

(c) Lamp 1212. Eros. Made in Cyprus, found at Salamis. 3rd century A.D.

(d) Lamp 68 6-20 180. Goddess with double axe. Found at Ephesus. Made at Athens. Early 4th century A.D.

(e) Lamp 1226. Apollo. Made in Egypt, found at Behnesa. 3rd century A.D.

(f) Lamp 1356. Made at Athens. Found at Ephesus. Signed ΧΙΟΝΗ. First half of the 5th century A.D.

Plate 14

(a) Lamp 1913 10-14 4. 'Candlestick lamp'. Made in Palestine. Nonsense inscription. 5th century A.D. (Department of Medieval and Later Antiquities).

(b) Lamp 1334. Horse. Made in Cyprus. *Circa* 5th century A.D. Signed ΕΥΤΥΧΗΤΟΣ.

(c) Lamp 1962 9-20 2. Made in Italy in the 3rd or 4th century A.D.

(d) Lamp EC 819. 'Frog Lamp'. Made in Egypt. 3rd or 4th century A.D. (Department of Medieval and Later Antiquities).

(e) Lamp 66 1-1 316. Made in Syria? From Cyprus.
About 6th century. A.D. (Department of Medieval and Later Antiquities).

(f) Lamp EC 858 Early Christian. Made in Italy. *Circa* 6th or 7th century A.D. (Department of Medieval and Later Antiquities).

Plate 15

(a) Lamp 1326. Pan and woman. Made in western Asia Minor. Found at Calymnos. 5th-6th century A.D.

(b) Lamp 56 8-26 206. Cross. Made in western Asia Minor. Found at Calymnos. 5th-6th century A.D.

(c) Lamp 67 11-22 232. Man and woman. Made in western Asia Minor. Found at Ephesus. 5th-6th century A.D.

(d) Lamp 70 1-5 19. Made in western Asia Minor. Found in a Lydian tumulus at Sardis. 6th-7th century A.D.

(e) Lamp 22829. Made in Upper Egypt. 7th to 8th century A.D. (Egyptian Department).

Plate 16

(a) Lamp 1402. Upper mould for lamp similar to pl. 5c. Found at Ephesus.

(b) Lamp 1401. Lower mould for lamp. Made in Athens. Late 1st century A.D., into the 2nd century.

(c) Lamp 1400. Upper mould for lamp. Made in Egypt. Found at Naukratis. 3rd to 4th century A.D.

(d) Lamp 1498. Mass of lamps fused together. Ephesian fabric, probably found at Ephesus. Second half of the 1st century, into the 2nd century A.D.

(e) Lamp 1497. As (d) above.

Colour Plates

Plate A
Lamp 249. Athenian lamp, found at Tocra in Cyrenaica. End of the 5th century B.C.

Plate B
Lamp 398. Two-nozzled lamp supported by a figure of Bes. Made in Egypt. 1st century A.D. (Egyptian Department).

Plate C
Lamp 1925 10-16 1. In the form of a gladiator's helmet. Made in Italy. Signed FORTIS. About A.D. 100.
Lamp 442. Green-glazed lamp in helmet form. Made at Cologne, where it was found. About A.D. 200.

Plate D
Lamp EC 716. 'African lamp'. Bust of a woman. 5th century A.D. (Department of Medieval and Later Antiquities).

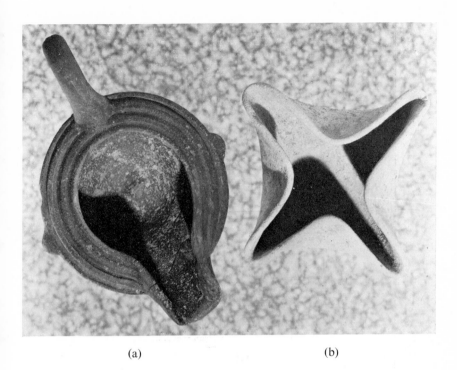

(a)   (b)

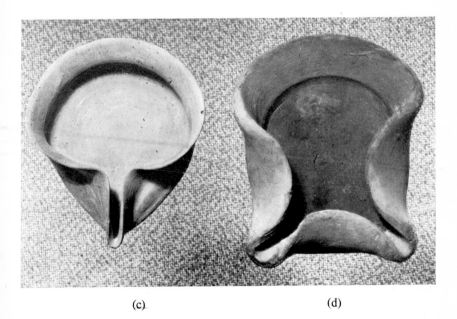

(c)   (d)

Plate 1

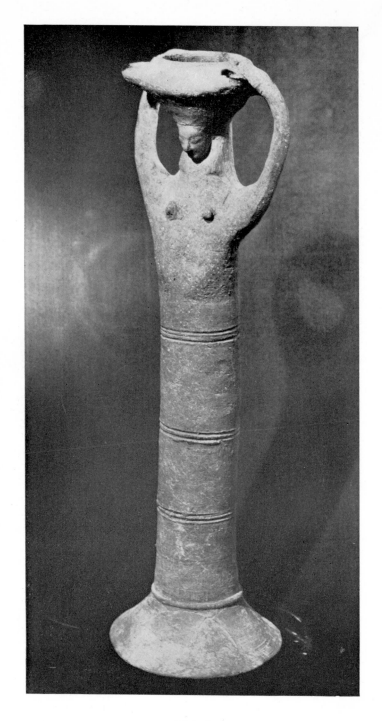

Plate 2

(a)   (b)   (c)

(d)   (e)   (f)

Plate 3

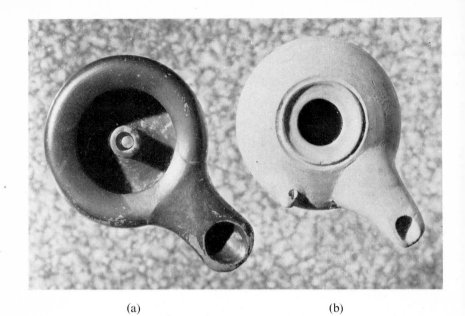

(a)   (b)

(c)   (d)   (e)

Plate 4

(a)

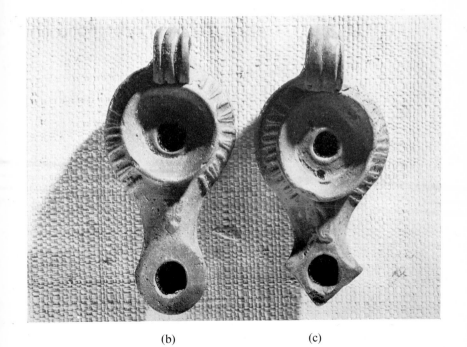

(b)   (c)

Plate 5

(a)   (b)   (c)

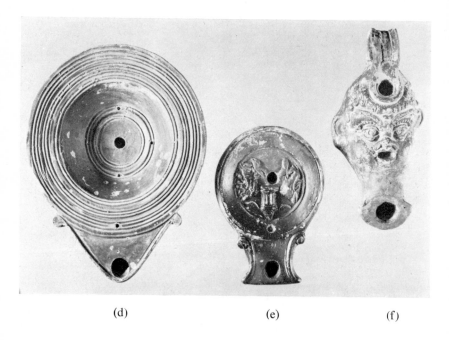

(d)   (e)   (f)

Plate 6

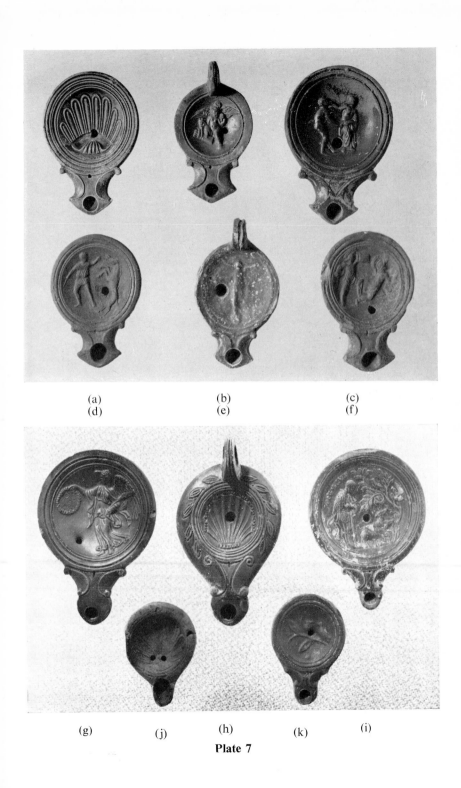

(a)   (b)   (c)
(d)   (e)   (f)

(g)   (j)   (h)   (k)   (i)

Plate 7

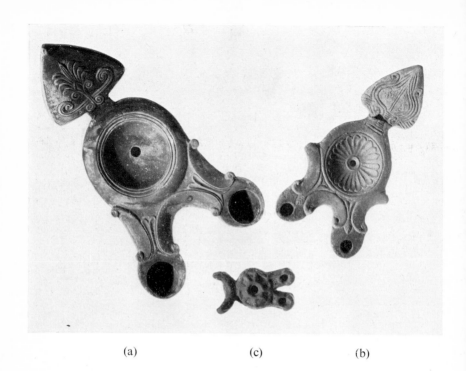

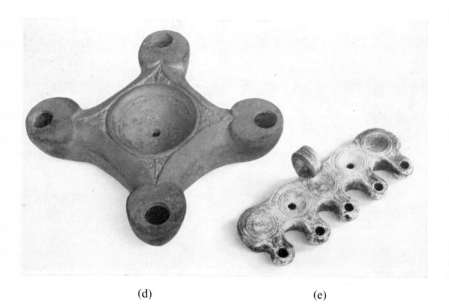

(a) (c) (b)

(d) (e)

Plate 8

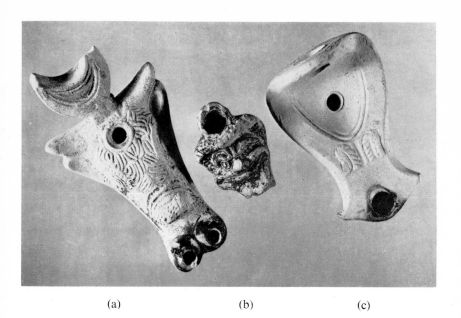

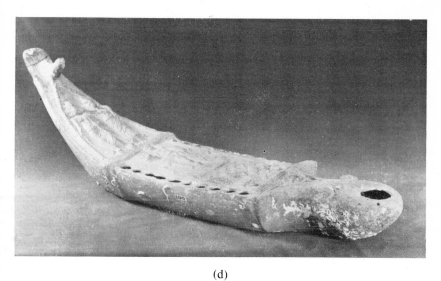

Plate 9

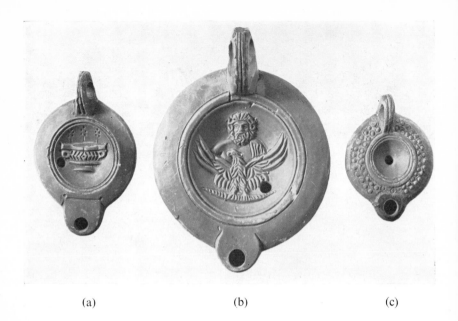

(a)   (b)   (c)

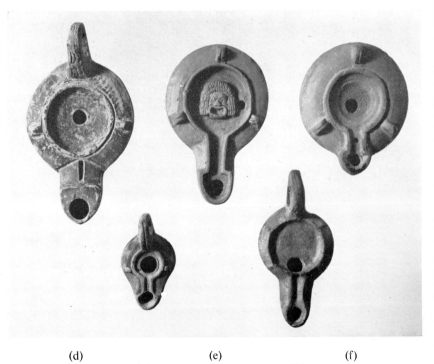

(d)   (e)   (f)

      (g)   (h)

Plate 10

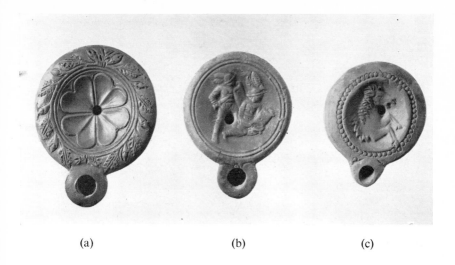

(a)   (b)   (c)

(d)   (e)   (f)

Plate 11

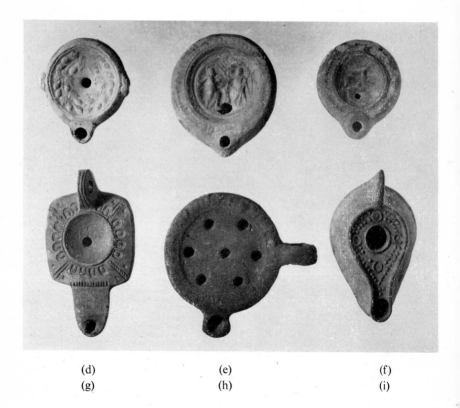

(a)   (b)   (c)

(d)   (e)   (f)

(g)   (h)   (i)

Plate 12

| (a) | (b) | (c) |
| (d) | (e) | (f) |

Plate 13

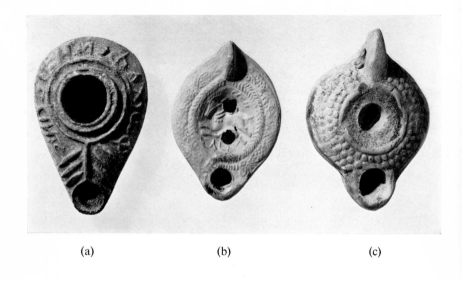

(a)   (b)   (c)

(d)   (e)   (f)

Plate 14

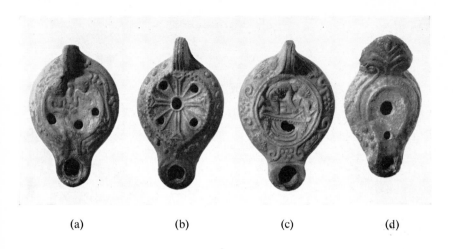

(a) (b) (c) (d)

(e)

Plate 15

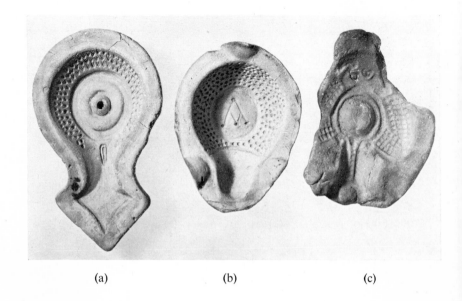

(a)　　　　　　　(b)　　　　　　　(c)

(d)　　　　　　　　　　(e)

Plate 16